SPIRITUAL WARFARE MANUAL

Mickey Bonner

P.O. Box 90593, Houston, Texas 77290

Printed in the United States of America

ISBN 1-878578-02-2

This volume is dedicated
to my wonderful grandchildren,
Lowell and Nicole Parker,
who were sent by God
into our family and who
have brought an even deeper revelation
of His wondrous love
for both my wife,
Margaret, and me.

Table of Contents

Chapter One

Can a Christian Have a Demon?

Perhaps one of the most controversial questions asked today is, "Can a Christian have a demon?" The biblical answer is yes. In order to develop this teaching, it must be first established what biblical ground rules Satan must follow. By that I mean, because of the blood of Jesus and His sacrificial life, our enemy has lost his power. He can only operate up to the blood of Jesus. From there on, he is powerless. However, the Scripture teaches that Satan does have a power to work in the Christian. So I will deal with the Bible doctrine in this area.

First, let me establish the fact that I will not deal in deliverance with a lost person except from the standpoint of breaking the blindness as mentioned in II Corinthians 4:3-4 in order that the unsaved person can see the light of the gospel and be saved. The reason for this is that a lost person cannot hold his deliverance. However, when an individual has trusted Christ, then his body becomes the temple of God. At that point, all that is Christ will be placed within him. It is through this enabling power that he can move and have his being. Satan was completely defeated at Calvary. Therefore when a person confesses his sins in true repentance, giving himself to Christ and inviting Him in, the power of the enemy is stripped. However, in order to overcome the enemy, we must learn to appropriate that power.

To begin this study we must understand what the enemy can do through wiles to defeat the Christian and demonize him. First, what does this word, demonize, mean?

To make it as simple as possible, it is the Christian who has given place to the devil and has received into his flesh unclean spirits. Incidentally, it is my personal belief that the way most Christians are overcome is through their mouths — not by what goes into the mouth — but by what comes out. The quickest way to lose a righteous relationship with Christ is to be negative through confession. The Bible teaches that it is not what goes into a person's mouth that defiles him, but what comes out.

Now regarding carnal or fleshly man — it is through him that Satan sets up his activity. He is easily demonized because of his powerless resistance to the enemy. What is carnal man? He is much spoken of in the Word, especially by Paul. Carnality is the activity of the flesh (Christian man) trying to consume and dominate the Spirit (Christ in you the hope of glory). This is found in Galatians 5:17-21. If Satan has to loose you to Christ in salvation, he will then begin to direct his demon forces to bind the child of God to a form of godliness, but to deny the power thereof. Now this does not mean to deny the virgin birth, the blood atonement, the basic truths of the Word, but to bring that person to the place of dependence upon the flesh or the activity thereof, rather than upon God's Spirit and His revelation. Carnality is feeling and not faith. It is activity without revelation. It is pride and not self-denial. The classic Scriptures for this teaching are found in I Corinthians 3:1-5 and Romans 8:5-8.

In the Corinthian account we are shown the activity and personality of the carnal mind. Paul says in I Corinthians 3:1, KJV: "And I, brethren, could not speak unto you as unto spiritual, but as unto carnal, even as unto babes in Christ." Then in verse 3 he uses the word, carnal, and develops it by saying, "For ye are yet carnal: for whereas there is among you envying, and strife, and divisions, are ye not carnal, and walk as men?" The unique position of these verses is that although the word, carnal, is used twice, it is not the same word in the Greek. The first carnal (verse 1) means acting like babies; wanting your way in everything. The second carnal (verse 3) is the adverb which means fleshly, or totally given over to the flesh. Again, Satan works in the flesh by causing envy, divisions, anger, etc., until it becomes uncontrollable. In fact, a good rule of thumb is: anything you can control is flesh, but anything that controls you is spirit. There are only two kinds of spirit. Flesh out of control is spirit manifestation.

We find the same position in Romans 8 in that

the flesh cannot please God. In fact, it is enmity against God. This, simplified, means it is hostile to God. So the beginning step of demonization is flesh out of control. Again, the slide very likely begins as a negative confession.

Make a study of Galatians 5:17-21. Herein lies the major point. The flesh would, if it could, control the spirit, and the spirit would, if you and I allowed, control the flesh. The Christian chooses whom he will serve (Romans 6:16).

Demons move into the flesh once the beachhead or stronghold is established and the deterioration of the Christian's walk begins. In regard to that — what Isaiah 14 says must not be forgotten — that Satan will not open his prison house. The Christian, to be set free, therefore must have deliverance.

Let's look at the way our confession opens the door to demonization. In James 3:6, KJV, it says,

> "And the tongue is a fire, a world of iniquity: so is the tongue among our members, that it defileth the whole body, and setteth on fire the course of nature; and it is set on fire of hell."

Our confession not only directs our lives, but causes possession, and in the Christian's case, demonization.

In the complete study of this chapter, we find that the course of nature is set by our confession. Someone has well said, "You are what you say." If demons can cause you to be critical or negative or to curse, you open yourself up to infestation. In fact, that chapter establishes that sweet and bitter water will not come from the same well. It also teaches the Christian in the fourteenth and fifteenth verses:

> "But if ye have bitter envying and strife in your hearts, glory not, and lie not against the truth. This wisdom descendeth not from above, but is earthly, sensual, devilish."

There are two things here: first, in this chapter on the tongue, God says a person that speaks the positive (about Christ) and then is negative (against man), does not speak from above (revelation). In fact, his Christian walk is a lie in that he lies against the truth (Jesus). Second, God says about the critical Christian in this chapter that the wisdom he shows is not from God's Holy Spirit, but from another spirit. He says that this person is earthly (humanistic), sensual (from the flesh reasoning), devilish or, from another translation, demoniacal. Said another way, it means speaking by a spirit controlling the person's mind and mouth. Again it must be understood that James is dealing with the Christian.

Famous in Syria

There are many Scriptures that deal with the word, demonized. In Matthew 4:23-25, KJV, we find regarding Christians and demons:

> "Jesus went about all Galilee, teaching in their synagogues, and preaching the gospel of the kingdom, and healing all manner of sickness and all manner of disease among the people. And His fame went throughout all of Syria: and they brought unto Him all sick people that were taken with divers diseases and torments, and those which were possessed with devils, and those which were lunatick, and those that had the palsy; and He healed them. And there followed Him great multitudes of people from Galilee, and from Decapolis, and from Jerusalem, and from Judaea, and from beyond Jordan."

Here the Scripture uses the word which, in the Greek, means demonized or controlled in areas by Satan.

Also Matthew 8:16, KJV:

> "When the even was come, they brought unto Him many that were possessed with devils: and He cast out the spirits with His word, and healed all that were sick."

Again, these were under the power of demons. That's what it means to be demonized.

What are demons? We will touch on this later; however, I personally feel they are fallen angels that followed after Satan in his rebellion toward God (Isaiah 14; Ezekiel 28). Their goal throughout history has been (and will always be) to seek residence in the physical. In fact, one translation teaches in Ephesians 6:12 that they are persons without bodies. I believe this, having had unique experiences in the area of deliverance. They do demonstrate individuality. They are evil, vile, and filthy. In fact, it could best be said that they are the opposite of God, Christ and the angels. But, best of all, the evil one and his fallen angels were defeated at Calvary by the life, death, resurrection and blood of Jesus Christ!

Another example of demons controlling an individual is found in the Old Testament in the Scriptures dealing with King Saul and David. Saul had working within his flesh the forces of evil. These demons could only be quelled and disarmed by David's soothing music. However, eventually Saul was demonized and brought to the place of trying to kill God's servant, David. Being totally influenced and captured by the spirits within him, he was finally driven to commit the "sin unto death." This happened when he endeavored to make contact with demons themselves. Saul sought counsel from anyone who could contact the dead for him. One was found for him, and he went in secret. His desire was to speak to the deceased prophet, Samuel. A witch is one with a familiar spirit (demon) who controls her life. For this rebellion against God, Saul lost his life the next day. This is found in I Samuel 28:7-25; I Chronicles 10:13-14. Saul was an Old Testament believer and a classic case of demonization. In fact, Saul experienced the three evidences of being a believer: (1) chastisement of God moving on his circumstances, (2) scourging of the physical (Hebrews 12:3-7), and (3) finally, death that always comes when a child of God keeps on rebelling against God (Proverbs 29:1).

Let's Sell the House

Another case of Christians having demons is in God's account of the New Testament Church in Jerusalem. The power of Christ's life had exploded into the lives of the believers — so much so that they had experienced the transformed life that is promised to everyone who is saved. They especially experienced the death-to-self concept. The basic nature of the Jew is to possess and have ownership; the nature of the Spirit-controlled person is to give of himself or of that which he owns. Such was the experience of these newly filled Christians. They became so like Christ that they sold what they possessed and brought the proceeds to the church to be given to those who had need. Now in that exciting, Spirit-charged atmosphere of revival, there was a couple whose names were Ananias and Sapphira. Having seen firsthand the power of God, they decided between themselves to sell their possessions and bring the money to the church for distribution. However, after the property was sold, Satan moved into their lives. They lost total faith in God in the matter of their giving. In essence, they decided to withhold a part of the money for themselves; yet when turning the money in, they represented themselves as having given all. The problem was that they not only lied to the congregation, but to God also.

Ananias was the first to take his offering to the church. When he approached Peter with his gift, the Holy Spirit impressed Peter that this man was misrepresenting what he was doing. Peter's statement was,

> "Ananias, why hath Satan filled thine heart to lie to the Holy Ghost, and to keep back part of the price of the land? While it remained, was it not thine own? and after it was sold, was it not in thine own power? why hast thou conceived this thing in thine heart? thou hast not lied unto men, but unto God" (Acts 5:3-4, KJV).

The Bible teaches that at that moment Ananias fell to the floor dead (Acts 5:5).

Later his wife entered the room to bring her part of the offering. Peter asked her if she had sold the land for so much. She said, "Yes." Then Peter replied, "The young men who have just buried your husband are coming in the door at this moment." Sapphira at that moment died. They were an example of demonized Christians. They gave place and demons entered and took control, even to the point of Satan filling their hearts and lying against the Holy Spirit. Ananias and Sapphira were demonized Christians.

Going further in this area, we find in Galatians 3:1-2, KJV:

> "Oh foolish Galatians, who hath bewitched you, that ye should not obey the truth, before whose eyes Jesus Christ hath been evidently set forth, crucified among you? This only would I learn of you, Received ye the Spirit by the works of the law, or by the hearing of faith?"

And in Galatians 4:3 we read, "Even so we, when we were children, were in bondage under the elements of the world."

The word, bewitched, in Galatians 3:1 is a translation from the Greek that means bringing evil on one by praise; evil eye; to charm or bewitch one. It also hints of those who led away others into error by witchcraft. In another translation it speaks of a magician having hypnotized and cast an evil spell on them. The Scripture also teaches that their minds have been clouded. The Greek word, bascamia, means bewitched, or another way to say it is demonized. These Christians had given place to demon forces in their lives.

Looking further in I Timothy 4:1, KJV, we read, "Now the Spirit speaketh expressly, that in the latter times some shall depart from the faith, giving heed to seducing spirits, and doctrines of devils." Here is biblical prophecy of Christians being seduced and demonized. Paul tells Timothy that in the latter times Christians shall depart from the faith, giving heed or taking in seducing spirits and doctrines of devils — so relevant is this in these end times! How easily seduced are Christians today (to partake in the emotional rather than the spiritual). Satan attacks today to destroy the line of revelation that comes from the Holy Spirit to the believer. Through carnality there is strife and contention constantly in Christendom. These are Satan's efforts to keep the Kingdom of God decimated and powerless. The demons are constantly active in the lives or against the lives of Christians. For example, giving heed to seducing spirits means allowing them to come in. They take up residence in the physical and fight constantly to hold their prey (in this case the "body, the temple of God"). Dear Christian, how important it is for us to understand the working of Satan against our lives! We will be dealing later with the principle of the armour of God and the defense we have in the blood of Christ. However, we must not forget that the weapons of our warfare are not carnal, and we must never forget that the enemy we face is invisible and seeking to destroy us. We must learn and know with settled and absolute knowledge that the demons are defeated by the blood of Jesus and that we are more than conquerors. We have total victory in Jesus Christ! To appropriate this we must act the part.

Chapter Two

Breaking Genetic Ties

Perhaps one of the most unusual experiences in deliverance is in the area of genetic ties. I stumbled onto this in a prayer session years ago. I had been familiar with the Old Testament Scriptures that state that the sins of the father are visited on the children of the third and fourth generation. However, I had never dealt with this area. As I was praying with a person, I prayed to break these ties from the womb. Something happened in the individual. There was a release. We began to deal with this more extensively in these sessions and found that many experienced great relief in areas of bondage. I now incorporate this into every session.

I cannot explain it other than somehow Satan can influence the life as it is given. This was brought home to me recently when in an article I read how babies adopted into families that were happy and stable, even into Christian environments, would in many cases as adults, revert to the life-style experienced by their biological parents. In many cases, these children who were never around alcohol or drugs were in their early adult years drawn irresistibly to this bondage. Again, let me state that these areas can be broken when dealt with in deliverance praying. In this case, when I pray with a person, I renounce his genetic ties and then agree with him in prayer until there is release. We have seen profound changes in many who have gone through this quiet prayer experience.

Also, I have noticed unusual changes in those with ethnic backgrounds. Before I share this with you, you must understand that this is my personal experience in ministry. I urge you not to speak or preach on this subject because there is no Scriptural precedent. Stay with the Bible in every matter. However, I will share several illustrations in dealing with ethnic backgrounds.

To begin with, I have discovered in many with Indian heritage the need for breaking of ties. I feel this is due to the background of spiritism practiced by many tribes. I have heard many stories from those who are tribal members of "experiences," especially in the area of healing. One man of Indian heritage with whom I ministered in Espanola, New Mexico, explained how he was healed by a tribal medicine man. However, he spoke of great spiritual bondage from that moment on in his life. When I prayed with him there was much release in the area of witchcraft. Over the years, I have ministered to many of Indian background and have seen great release in breaking of genetic ties, sometimes even to a change of personality.

Another ethnic area is in the line of those who

lived in Africa or in the Caribbean islands. In these areas of the world, witchcraft is a life-style, therefore bringing a habitation of demons in the flesh. Several years ago, I was asked to minister to a teenage girl who had been born in Jamaica. Her parents were deep into the practice of witchcraft that involved the sacrifice of chickens and other living things. Her mother told her later that before she was born, she had been dedicated to Satan. In due process of time, as a young girl, she was brought to America and adopted by a wonderful Christian family. However, as she grew into mid-teens she began to act strangely, even to the phenomenon that involved demonic powers. She did not want these things in her life. Her adoptive parents sought to help her in every way, but to no avail. These manifestations would still surface. Finally, they brought her to one of our meetings and asked if I would deal with her need. As I began to ask God for guidance, I was strongly impressed to pray for genetic ties to be broken. It took some while in warfare, but finally this area was broken. We then dealt with her in salvation, and from there for the rest of her bondage to be broken. God set her free!

Let me urge you that are ministering in this area to always pray to break genetic ties in the person with whom you are dealing. This will release them from the negative attributes that followed the genes in the flesh, as well as the D.N.A. programming in the nature, color, abilities and body formation that come with birth and growth.

Again, the only doctrine we have as a precedent for this is the several verses that express the "sins of the fathers." Don't preach this; however, use it in your prayers to bring deliverance.

Spoken Word of Curse

I first became aware that words were power a number of years ago. I had made a study of the confession from the area of criticism and negative confession. In so doing, I became convinced that not only did our confession bind or loose our own lives, but acted in the same way upon the lives of others. As I studied the verse in James 3:6, it spoke of the tongue setting on fire the course of nature (the world is directed by what is said). In other words, as "men wax worse and worse," their negative confession brings further degradation on all humanity. The Bible teaches that words are power. This was further brought home to me as I read Watchman Nee's book, *Latent Power of the Soul.* In his writing, he tells of a missionary who began to experience illness. Nothing could be done to correct his condition. Finally, one day he discovered that a group of well-meaning Christians were praying against him. He immediately counteracted their straight-line prayers by cancelling them out by the blood of Jesus Christ. He was immediately healed!

Now, praying in a straight line is another message entirely. However, let me urge you to never pray directly to anyone. The reason for this is that the soul of an individual has great power. This has been demonstrated many times through powers expressed by those who are involved in meditation or other mind control activities. There is an inner power that, when harnessed by Satan, can be used in an unusual way. However, the penalty for this is possession, and eventually, complete separation from God for eternity (Genesis 6:3). Better said, they will spend eternity in hell. Because of the soul having power when there is prayer aimed directly to an individual, it will bring change in many cases. However, it is not by the power of God. We must go to God in the name of Jesus in dealing with anyone through prayer. In this we use the power of God which brings not only victory, but also establishes God's plan and purpose through intercession.

The Mummy's Curse

Now in the light of the mind, spoken words also contain power. There are many verses in Scripture that deal with this subject. For example, "Out of the abundance of the heart the mouth speaketh." In other words, what you say is what you are. It is an exhausting study to look up in the concordance the word, say, then run the references. You will be astounded at how much the words declared from our lips have to do with power. It is because of this that when I deal in deliverance, it is always imperative to break the spoken word of curse. In fact, the way I pray with the person is to say, "Father, I declare broken all curses spoken about or by this person." Then something always happens to the life with which we are dealing. Now I know when I use the word, curse, in writing this, that there will be all kinds of thoughts crossing the average person's mind. Perhaps you feel it only applies to mummies on Saturday afternoon's movies on television — or maybe memories of novels regarding black practices of weird people of ages past visiting the twentieth century through being resurrected by evil powers. No, that is not what I mean. Your words are power, and when you speak in a negative way about yourself or others, you set the course of life with this declaration. For example, have you ever made the statement upon waking in the morning: "It's going to be one of those days." Guess what? You were right. It will be unless you break that confession. I know this is unusual doctrine, but it works in deliverance.

Physician, Heal Thyself

Several years ago, I experienced a very heartbreaking situation. It involved an experience with a pastor and a church. Through it all, God not only advanced our ministry, but brought us to a much deeper trust in God and strengthened my Christian life. I praise Him for the wonderful experience of breaking that was involved. At first, because of the hurt involved, we were numb. Then we began to feel great oppression atmospherically.

It was on my family, in our home and all around our lives. However, after a while the truths of Christ began to glimmer through in times of our revival meetings and in moments of prayer and especially during ministry sessions with others in the area of deliverance. Then, one day I suddenly realized what was happening to us — negative confession toward us by others. I now realized the position of "Physician, heal thyself." I began to pray to break these forces toward my family, my ministry and my own life. It worked! We were released!

Please remember, as in dealing with Satan, it is not a one-time, once-for-all experience. You must enter into warfare daily. In fact, the Bible teaches, "Submit yourselves therefore to God. Resist the devil, and he will flee from you" (James 4:7, KJV). We resist as we submit. I urge you to deal in the area of breaking the spoken word of curse as you pray for yourself and for others, and see the change. It works! Your words are power! So are the words of others toward you.

Chapter Three

Pulling Down Strongholds

In this chapter I am going to reestablish the need of breaking bondage in the individual life, and from there, the ability to pray for someone else in that same capacity. I will be repeating several things that we have already covered in this writing. However, I think that it is well said that repetition is the greatest form of learning.

Now to enter into the ministry of deliverance there must be, first of all, a total cleansing of one's personal life in order to not only have authority over spirit beings, but at the same time not to be overcome by them. To begin with, we are going to share how there must be a personal cleansing within in order to receive the power and authority that are necessary. I cannot establish strong enough the fact that to bring principalities to attention and to obedience, there must be the dealing with sin in one's own personal life. To begin with, there must be the facing of every issue of the past. If there is unforgiveness, it must be dealt with, for the Bible teaches that if you do not forgive others their trespasses, your trespasses cannot be forgiven you. In the light of this, the Bible specifically states in Psalm 66:18, KJV: "If I regard iniquity in my heart, the Lord will not hear me." Again the word, regard, means to know that it is there and not deal with it. Isaiah 59:2, KJV, states, "But your iniquities have separated between you and your God, and your sins have hid His face from you, that He will not hear." So to bring yourself to biblical authority there must be that personal confession within.

Broken Wire

Unconfessed sin stands as a broken wire from the source of power. The power is there, but in order for it to be coupled, there must be the mending of the heart. There must be the reestablishing of righteousness (which means right standing with God). There must be the edifying (building up) of the spiritual life by constant pursuit of Christ. We are commanded to enter into warfare, and in so doing we are promised that the weapons of our warfare are not carnal, but mighty through God to the pulling down of strongholds. In dealing with one's own personal life, there are biblical conditions for deliverance. First of all there must be humility on our part. The Bible says in James 4:6-7, KJV:

> "But He giveth more grace. Wherefore He saith, God resisteth the proud, but giveth grace unto the humble. Submit yourselves therefore to God. Resist the devil, and he will flee from you."

In God's conditions, He shares that the proud person has no power in Christ. In fact, there is resistance from God to that person of pride. It was because of pride that Satan had his downfall and was cast out of Heaven. The five "I wills" of Isaiah 14 are all full of pride. In Ezekiel 28 we again discover that pride was the reason for the fall of Satan from Heaven. Proverbs states: "Pride goeth before destruction, and an haughty spirit before a fall" (Proverbs 16:18, KJV).

One Through Five

Continuing in James 4:7, it tells us that our power comes by submitting to God. In fact, the level of our submission to God is our level of resistance to Satan. It is the power of God that destroys the devil's influence. So then to enter into the ministry of deliverance, there must first be humility. With humility comes brokenness in the life of the person in order that he might operate in the power of God flowing through him. Second, there must be open honesty. For a person to have ministry in the area of breaking the bondage of Satan, he must be absolutely open with his life. The Bible says in Psalm 32:5-6:

> "I acknowledged my sin unto thee, and mine iniquity have I not hid. I said, I will confess my transgressions unto the Lord; and thou forgavest the iniquity of my sin. Selah. For this shall every one that is godly pray unto Thee in a time when Thou may-

est be found: surely in the floods of great waters they shall not come nigh unto Him."

Again for God's power to manifest itself to the person who is ministering deliverance, there must be open honesty.

Third, there must be confession. There must be the facing of the issues of the personal life and then claiming God's freedom from these issues through confession. The Bible says in I John 1:9, KJV: "If we confess our sins, He is faithful and just to forgive us our sins, and to cleanse us from all unrighteousness."

Fourth, the individual must renounce sin totally. He must be willing to stand against it completely and bring himself to a cleansed state by the Word and by the blood of Jesus Christ. Again, for spirits to be dealt with, there must be a pure heart speaking the will of God. Demons are not terrified of people — they are terrified of the blood of Jesus Christ and the work of the cross. They were defeated by the blood of the Lamb, and for the Christian to represent the blood there must be the purity of the heart and the cleansing of the life. This comes only in the renouncing of sin. In another area of Scripture, Proverbs 28:13, KJV, we read, "He that covereth his sins shall not prosper: but whoso confesseth and forsaketh them shall have mercy." If we deal with the sin in our lives openly, we can at that point be brought to a place of power to represent God's kingdom and authority in the lives and circumstances of those in demon bondage. Christ has all authority given Him under heaven and earth.

Fifth, there must be forgiveness on the part of the Christian toward any person who has ever harmed or hurt him. To harbor a root of bitterness negates all power that you have. The vast majority of all Christians will never be able to enter into the ministry of deliverance because of harbored bitternesses they have toward other people that have moved against them in some way. Holding on to resentment means to stand without being cleansed in the presence of the enemy and being there without the covering of the armour (Ephesians 6:10-17). The Bible says in Hebrews 12:15, KJV: "Looking diligently lest any man fail of the grace of God; lest any root of bitterness springing up trouble you, and thereby many be defiled." Now the root of bitterness goes deep into the personality of the individual; thereby overcoming any authority that he has. The problem is that in the root of bitterness there is the fruit of bitterness, which again has its foundation built in most cases upon pride. Therefore, to enter into the ministry of deliverance, one must forgive any person who has ever harmed or hurt him. One of the best ways that I've found to deal with unforgiveness comes from a former missionary to China. Her statement was that every Christian ought to sit down with a sheet of paper and list all the negative things that have ever happened to him in his life. And upon having listed those, he should draw a line through each one as he praises God for the experiences. This brings release and freedom to the life. Then there is a need to go back and make a list of people who have been harmed or hurt by your life and go through the same position of confession. Where there is release, then there is victory. Where there is no release, then there is a need to contact that person if possible and close the door of bitterness through praying with him, if he allows. Just a move for restitution breaks the bondage of the enemy. Again, forgiveness is a key to power; it is the door to grace; it is the formula for answered prayer. The Bible states in many places that if there is no forgiveness, there is no answered prayer. In the model prayer we are shown this. "Forgive us our trespasses as we forgive those who trespass against us." Another translation says, "Forgive us our debts as we forgive our debtors." How important it is to realize that Satan brings bondage and hindrance to our lives through these areas of unforgiveness!

Place of Power

And then last, but not least, to enter into the place of power, there must be the claiming of God's promise. That is found in Joel 2:32, KJV: "And it shall come to pass, that whosoever shall call on the name of the Lord shall be delivered. . . ." God deals at that place to bring victory. We have the promise that we can have deliverance from bondage. However, in the course of deliverance, the formula must be followed, and each step must be progressively taken to bring personal release to the life. For it is only when one is cleansed that he can enter into the ministry of deliverance; only then can that individual stand in the place of authority using the blood of Jesus Christ to release others from evil incarceration. Never forget that the Christian has four sources of power that can be used. The first source is the cross. Colossians 2:15, KJV, says, "And having spoiled principalities and powers, He made a shew of them openly, triumphing over them in it." Now that simply means that when Christ died on the cross and rose from the grave, He openly showed the authority that He had. We, in Him, have identically the same power because it is His life through ours that can spoil principalities. Also in Hebrews 2:14-15, KJV:

> "Forasmuch then as the children are partakers of flesh and blood, He also Himself likewise took part of the same; that through death He might destroy him that had the power of death, that is, the devil; and deliver them who through fear of death were all their lifetime subject to bondage."

The power is in the cross of Christ.

The second source of power is the blood of Christ. We find in Revelation 12:11, KJV: "And they overcame him by the blood of the Lamb and by the word of their testimony; and they loved not their lives unto the death." What a marvelous promise that through the substitutionary death of Christ on the cross, not only did He bring us eternal life, but He gave us authority to be released in our lives and to pray in warfare praying and release others! The blood of Jesus is not only our grace, our salvation, our life, but it is also the source of our power.

Third, the name of the Lord is given to us as a source of power. In Proverbs 18:10, KJV, the Bible says, "The name of the Lord is a strong tower: the righteous runneth into it, and is safe." How many times in warfare we have used the phrase, "Praise the Lord" or "Jesus is Lord" only to see spirits tremble in the lives of those with whom we are dealing! The name, Jesus, is above every name given to us, for there is no other name under heaven whereby man can be saved — the glorious name of Jesus — Jesus Christ our sovereign Saviour and Lord! He is our life, our breath, our being, and our personal victory! He is our overcomer! He is our deliverer — Jesus!

Fourth is the Word itself, which is Christ Himself, according to John 1:1-2. However, in dealing in spiritual warfare the Bible says in Matthew 4, in the temptation of Christ, that Christ constantly used the Word, itself, as an offensive weapon against Satan. His statement was, "It is written." In all of Satan's temptations the Word, itself, stood stalwart against his power. The greatest strength in spiritual warfare comes from daily Bible study. I liken it to a battery in an automobile . . . or a well-meaning person who wants to save his alternator, so he disconnects the fan belt to stop the wear and tear. In a sense, this is a sure way to keep from having to buy a new alternator, for if there is no use of the part, then it is going to survive. However, the problem is that if there is not a constant source of power going into the battery, even though it will work at the outset, eventually the battery is going to be drained. The Word overcomes Satan and is to be used offensively. Now again I use the word, offense, rather than defense. Most of us think of our circumstances with the evil one as being a defensive position. However, we must be in the battle. Very few Christians ever know what it is to enter into spiritual warfare. Another verse of Scripture that deals with this is Ephesians 6:17, KJV: "And take the helmet of salvation, and the sword of the Spirit, which is the word of God." There is much teaching in the verses prior to that. However, we must realize that the helmet of salvation comes by God's revealed Word to the individual. God's pure revelation is given to the heart. How imperative it is for the child of God to stay constantly in the Word to keep the battery charged! He must know his authority over the enemy in order to experience what faith's position is in the life. Only through the study of the Word and daily submission of one's life comes that ultimate victory in Christ. Again, before the ministry of deliverance can be entered into, there must be personal relationship with Christ and the edification of the body in order to build the power source. It is never to be forgotten that the Christian has all authority against the enemy, and that authority has been given at the moment of salvation. Perhaps one of the things never realized by the child of God is that he is commanded to enter daily into warfare. The Word states that in II Timothy 2:4: "No man that warreth entangleth himself with the affairs of this life; that he may please Him who hath chosen him to be a soldier." Herein lies God's personal declaration regarding spiritual warfare. The tragedy is that so few ever enter therein. Unless a person is willing to deal with his own personal life and be brought clean, there cannot be that release. That goes for his life as well as those he prays for in deliverance.

Imagine That

Paul brings this home to us in II Corinthians 10:3-5, KJV. Here it states,

> "For though we walk in the flesh, we do not war after the flesh: (For the weapons of our warfare are not carnal, but mighty through God to the pulling down of strong holds;) casting down imaginations, and every high thing that exalteth itself against the knowledge of God, and bringing into captivity every thought to the obedience of Christ."

Here again are personal ground rules for victory. As stated in our other writings, God has shown me that the battlefield is prayer; the battleground is the mind. Now we do battle through prayer, whether it be audible, standing with someone against the binding of his heart, or dealing with our own minds. We are actually conducting warfare. Warfare, again, is taking God's power and will and putting it into a circumstance where Satan has brought bondage and bringing deliverance. Again, prayer is warfare. However, it must be understood that the Christian is incapable of dealing in the area of warfare if his own personal life is not right.

First, one must establish the need for deliverance. Many times this comes through an educational process as one reads the Word of God — one stands his or her life against the Word as a mirror and sees the reflection. No man will ever walk with God until he has been broken, and the best way to be broken is to ask God to reveal what He sees in your personal life. I have taught people to pray a prayer something like this, "Lord, reveal me to me as you see me." It is from that point that God establishes truth and brings the individual into a victorious walk. Now again, if you are wanting to enter into warfare, let's look at these verses we have just shared. God says that even though we walk in the flesh we do not war after the flesh. So many Scriptures deal with the area of complete submission to God. Therein lies the message of Philippians and Colossians; also of Romans, especially chapter 12:1-2. It is a total testimony of the fifteenth chapter of the book of John and the principle of the vine being Christ, the branches being us, and we are to make a constant effort to stay vitally united or grafted into that vine. We do that by pursuing the Lord. This will allow the fruit of Christ to be manifested through the life — after a period of brokenness or the tearing away of those superfluous things that will not stand in the shaking (Hebrews 12:27). That is called pruning.

Flesh Out of Control

Now, for a man to enter into the battle there must be the realization that he cannot walk in the flesh or be worldly and expect to have power with God. The Bible says that every Christian has a weapon. In the fourth verse of II Corinthians 10, KJV, it says, "For the weapons of our warfare. . . ." Now what are our weapons? Let's look at that again. Our weapons are the cross, the blood, the name of Jesus Christ and the Word of God. These can be used in authority after we have met the conditions for deliverance in our own lives. This comes through humility, honesty, confession, renouncing of sin, forgiveness and claiming God's promise. In essence, we have the power at the moment we are born again to enter into the conflict. However, it must be understood that the weapons that are given at the time of salvation can only be wielded from a posture of pure oneness with Christ. The Bible proclaims the warfare. Also, never forget that Satan, through wiles listed in Ephesians 6, is constantly trying to defeat and pull the Christian under. He is trying to destroy his walk, his welfare and his worship. If he can hinder one from hearing from God and from walking in the Spirit, he has accomplished his prime purpose. The reason is that the Christian who is in a powerless state is no threat to his dominion. But one who has learned his rights in Christ, and has learned that all authority comes from Jesus, can then overcome Satan. Therefore, he constantly battles the ongoing Christian, or better said the "going on" Christian — the one who desires through study, prayer and worship, a deeper, more perfect walk with Jesus Christ. Therefore, the weapon against Satan is the person of Christ, and the fact is established that Christians are in a warfare, for the word, warfare, in the fourth verse is a present tense position. It does not mean sometimes; it means all the time for the Christian. He is in a battle. Now in this case there is one of two positions he can hold. He is either a prisoner of war incarcerated with the vast majority of all Christians — those who are powerless, purposeless, without joy, without peace, and without liberty, or he is one of the very small number of people who have broken out of bondage and are choosing Christ that He might be manifested through their lives. These are in warfare and winning, for you see, there are no defensive positions for the Christian. He must be constantly on the offensive. As long as we are moving against Satan through prayer and Bible study, we are in God's perfect will. The minute we stop our frontal assault, the weight of all matters fall upon us and we are at that moment brought into bondage. Looking further into this Scripture, we find that it states, "For the weapons of our warfare are not carnal. . . ." I have dealt with the carnal position in a prior chapter. Finally, verse 4 says, ". . . to the pulling down of strong holds." Now a stronghold is that which Satan has effectively placed in the life of a Christian to defeat him. It can be anything — fear or lust, anger or pride — anything in the areas of flesh as listed in Galatians 5. Remember however, flesh out of control is spirit, so therefore a stronghold is that area that Satan has placed in the person to bring him to defeat. However, we have been given power to pull down the strongholds. The Christian can be liberated; can be set free. Satan is constantly working on the mind to hinder it, to bind it, developing hindrances and separation. Because of this the enemy runs rampant in the life of the individual, constantly keeping him under his circumstances — so much so that he is unable to get a word from God or to go on with God in prayer and developing authority in Jesus Christ's name. Paul, in writing this by inspiration of God, states that there has to be liberty coming from within. This can be an individual dealing with his own life or he can be brought to such authority in Christ that he can pray with others to break demonic bondage in their lives. Hence, this is what deliverance is all about — restoring relationship and fellowship with Christ. The fifth verse says, "Casting down imaginations, and every high thing that exalteth itself against the knowledge of God. . . ." Again, this is Satan dealing with the mind. You see, if Satan can cloud the mind of the individual and bring him to such a position that he cannot believe God, then the person is defeated. Paul is stating here that if persons will deal with the bondages that Satan has thrown into their lives, they can be brought to liberty. There is nothing in life bigger than God. He is Jehovah-Jireh; He will provide. He is Jehovah-Nissi, our Banner over us. He is Jehovah-Shalom, or Peace. He is Jehovah-Shammah, our beginning, our end. He is all-in-all, and all things were made by Him through Christ. Therefore, nothing can ever be brought upon us in this world without a way of escape having already been provided (I Corinthians 10:13).

Romans 8:28 is not a pressure valve, but is the actual purpose of Christ in the life of every individual. However, to be brought to victory, there must be the casting down of imaginations. That means that no matter what has happened or what the fears, they must be dealt with and thrown to the ground. Imagination is a built-up area of reason in the mind that tries to overcome the might of God. However, this is all that it is — imagination.

One night a well-meaning parent was dealing with his child who was terrified of the dark. He entered the room with a flashlight in his hand. The child lay trembling in terror. The father very wisely said, "Son, I am going to leave this light with you, and I want you, when you are afraid, to turn on this light and see that there is nothing in the dark that is not also in the light." There is no need to fear the dark. Fear is also a spirit. Perfect love casts out fear and perfect love is Jesus Christ alive in us.

In order to deal with fear, which is the major spirit problem (other than hatred) in the lives of most people, there must be a deep walk with Christ in one's personal life. For in that fifth verse of II Corinthians 10, it tells us that if anything negative has exalted itself above the knowledge of God and makes one act as if he cannot be free, it is imagination. God tells us that there must be the bringing of every thought into captivity to the obedience of Christ. How many times I have dealt with those whose minds were filled with uncontrollable thoughts! Quoting Scriptures, especially those of the blood of Jesus, filled those minds with the Word, and the bondages were completely broken. God says, "Wherefore gird up the loins of your mind . . ." (I Peter 1:13, KJV).

For deliverance to occur, the mind must be captured and presented to Christ. One does this by Scripture memorization and the pursuit of Christ with all one's heart. To minister to another person in the area of release from demonic activity, there must be the cleansing of one's own personal heart and dealing with matters of self. In so doing, it brings liberty that comes only through the power of the blood of Jesus Christ. Every Christian has the power to minister. However, to be defeated in the Christian life is to be defeated by an already defeated foe.

Chapter Four

The Ministry of Deliverance

Someone has said that America is being raped with occultism today. Most high schools have their own campus witches. A local county library offers summer seminars for junior high and high school students on the practice of witchcraft. A seventh grade teacher in a Dallas, Texas, public school required her students to draw their personal astrological signs and list the character traits of persons born under that sign. Leading universities offer accredited courses in witchcraft and the occult. Occult book sales have doubled in the last several years. There are over 25,000 paid astrologists in America. Anton LaVey's Satanic Church, which has congregations in most major American cities, boasts over 200,000 members. It is time for the Christian to enter into this warfare.

Angels Good and Bad

To finalize this book, I am going to share some areas that we must deal with after our own spiritual cleansing and preparation. We must have a working knowledge of the enemy. I believe Satan and his demons were formerly angels in heaven. According to the Bible, angels were assigned to various functions: warring, worshipping, ministering, guardianship, attending, and so forth. There are over 300 references to angels in the Scripture. They are known to be pure spirit beings, unlike man who is body, soul and spirit. Those who have completed a deep study in this area seem to refer to angels as being masculine. However, they are believed to be sexless, as well as ageless. There is no biblical reference as to their ability to reproduce. Their numbers are ten thousand times ten thousand plus thousands of thousands, as found in Revelation 5:11 and hundreds of millions as in Daniel 7:10. According to Hebrews 1:14, those who followed God have one direct purpose at this time, and that is to minister to the Christians (heirs of salvation).

Fallen angels are constantly moving against the Christian. Therefore it is imperative that there be a daily commitment of one's life to Christ. Without it there is no protection or authority to withstand Satan (Acts 19:13-17). The Bible teaches that there is grading of angels in the area of authority. Special angels are given the designation of "archangel" in the Scripture. Two of these are Gabriel and Michael. It is my belief that there was a third archangel named Lucifer. His name is Daystar, Son of the Morning, Bright and Shining One. Two references of his existence are in Ezekiel 28:12-19 and in Isaiah 14:12-17. The Scriptural passage that teaches that

Satan led a revolt in Heaven, and that he and one-third of the angels (stars) were cast out, is Revelation 12:4. When cast here on earth, his name was changed to Satan, Beelzebub, the devil, the accuser of God and His people (Job 1:7-8), and the adversary of God and good (I Peter 5:8). Hell will be the final abode for him and his followers according to Matthew 25:41. And it is also the final place of those who align themselves with him and his purposes.

I am going to give you some Scripture references to study. The Old Testament names for fallen angels are:

Evil Spirits	Judges 9:23 I Samuel 18:10; 19:9
Lying Spirits	I Kings 22:22-23 II Chronicles 18:21-22
Familiar Spirits	Leviticus 19:31 Leviticus 20:6, 27 Deuteronomy 18:11

The New Testament names for fallen angels are:

Foul and Unclean Spirits	Mark 9:25 Matthew 10:1 Revelation 18:2
Deaf and Dumb Spirits	Mark 9:17-21
Seducing Spirits	I Timothy 4:1

Evil Spirits	Acts 19:12, 15-16
Spirits of Infirmity	Luke 13:11
Spirits of Divination	Acts 16:16

The names given always indicate the tasks they have. They are highly organized, highly mobile and very powerful. One translation of Ephesians 6:12 says that they are invisible persons without bodies. Their prime purpose is to inhabit humanity and cause disaster. As we have said before they are filthy and intensely wicked. Christ gives us insight into this in Matthew 12:45. They are unredeemable, utterly without conscience or second thought.

They are supernaturally wicked and seem to share a hate for each other. They have superior intelligence due to witnessing generation after generation of humanity pass before them. They know how to manipulate and capture the human life in order to desecrate it. Man was made in the image of God, and this is their way of attacking God. They defeat through "wiles." The Bible speaks of this in Ephesians 6:11. An example of wiles is any situation where Satan knows how an individual will react to a circumstance, and he acts in order to defeat and pull down the Christian's walk. It can be in any area, but the object is to devastate the victory. The Bible says in Acts 10:38 that they bring sickness. In Matthew 4:24 they bring disease. In Luke 13:11 they want to cripple. In Matthew 12:22 they make blind and dumb. The Bible teaches that they hinder, torment and steal blessings from

God's children. Again, as we have said in the past, evil spirits give the opposite of the fruit of the Spirit of Galatians 5:22. They encourage lust, not love; depression, not joy; frustration, not peace; worry, not longsuffering; temper, not gentleness; evil, not goodness; and fear, not faith. In further study it is shown that they also counterfeit the spiritual gifts. They affect men especially in three ways. They cause demon oppression, which means to be pressed down, encumbered with, and bothered by an outside force of demonic spirits. They also bring demon possession which occurs when demon powers are in control of some part of an individual. Finally, they cause demon obsession, which is to be obsessed with or overly conscious of demonic spirits or evil.

Now this is not a Scriptural position. It is strictly a clinical observation of many who have had years of ministering in this area. Again, it must be stated that demons gain entrance into a person's life through willful sin and even unwillful sin (there are sins committed ignorantly and there is inherited sin which is genetically received). This is found in Deuteronomy 5:9; 28:46.

To Name a Few

Here are some of the sins by which demons can enter:

Gluttony: uncontrolled appetite
Poltergeist: ghosts
Hysteria: unnatural fear

Rebellion (I Samuel 15:23)
Adultery
Envy
Music (I Samuel 16:23, particularly rock or country & western)
Lying (I Kings 22:21-23)
Gambling
Pride
Self-pity
Unforgiveness (Matthew 6:14-15)
Doctrine of Error
Smoking
Homosexuality
Pornography
Illicit Sex
Dishonesty
Murder (including abortion)
Theft
Drug Abuse (legal and illegal)
Cheating
Fear
Traumatic Experience
Television
Movies: *The Exorcist,* etc.
Beverage Alcohol
Associations With People
Games: Dungeons and Dragons, Ouiji board and anything dealing in the spirit world
Profanity
Greed
Gossip

Uncontrollable Sin
No Spiritual Victory
Abnormal Passions
Chronic Emotional Turmoil
Addiction to Alcohol, Nicotine, Sex, Drugs, Vice
Introspection
Gluttony
Nervous and Apprehensive
Violent Temper
Instability
Fear
Intensely Spiritual

Steps to Bringing Deliverance

Having dealt with your own life to effect liberty and freedom, and having submitted yourself to the Lord, you can now begin to minister to others. Let's discuss the issues you are likely to be dealing with in someone's life. There are six areas that God has led me to in bringing deliverance.

First of all, NEGATIVE CONFESSION. I have already dealt with breaking all negative confession about them or by them and breaking all curses toward them, both spoken and also by "the abundance of the heart."

Second, I deal with GENETIC TIES. I ask God to break all genetic ties in the life of the person with his mother and father all the way back to Adam.

Third, I deal with SALVATION. I agree with God that the hindrance to salvation be broken. I do this with everyone in case one might be lost. This is imperative in the life of an individual. The tragedy today is that there is so much "easy believism" that the majority of problems in the lives of individuals in our churches begin with people having never been to Calvary with their lives and experienced the new birth (John 3:5). This was very graphically brought home to me recently when a friend conducted a revival meeting in one of the larger churches in Fort Worth, Texas. In the course of several services, the pastor was saved, the educational director was saved and the youth-music director was saved. I think the biggest move of Satan on the lives of individuals today is to bring them to a position of false salvation, thereby claiming their lives for eternity and destroying their relationship with God. So I agree with God for their salvation. If I am praying for a person apart from where I am at that moment, I pray not only for his salvation, but that laborers will be sent to bear testimony and witness to his soul that he might find Christ as his personal Saviour. The Scripture I use in this area is II Corinthians 4:3-4. In these verses it tells us the reason a person cannot be saved is because Satan has blinded his mind so that he cannot see the light of the gospel.

The next position I deal with after I have received releases from these first areas is in the area of HEALING. Now I do this because a great deal of infirmity in the lives of Christians is spirit-induced. So I pray in this manner: "Father, I agree with You that there be healing in the area of body, soul, spirit, mind, emotion and will." However, it must be understood that I deal with these one at a time, waiting for release in each area. Now in dealing with the soul and spirit, I am coming against scars that have been made in past experiences of life — for example, hostility, unforgiveness, roots of bitterness, etc. These areas must be claimed and cleansed that victory may come. From there, break bondage in the mind. The mind is an unusual instrument; it never forgets. It has basically two parts: the frontal lobe (reasoning areas in which men are faced with a moment-by-moment relationship to life) and the id (the vast subconscious of the mind which harbors all that has ever happened in one's past). This area, for the most part, is what is to be dealt with to break out the past forgotten areas that control a person in certain circumstances. However, I must urge you never to pray in a straight-line to the individual. It must never be forgotten that the mind has power and can be used of Satan even in deliverance to cause confusion. Always go to God in Jesus' name in your praying. Now here is how I conduct this part of the deliverance:

Let's Go to War

"Lord, I agree with You that the mind and id be cleansed and that every negative thing that has ever happened in the past (wherever it is hidden in the mind) be broken and hindrances be resolved; that all unforgiveness be washed away by the blood of Jesus all the way back through this life, through childhood and to birth through genetics on back to Adam." Be careful now. I realize that this may be strange; however, as we have prayed we have seen tremendous release in the lives of people whose minds have harbored negative things from the past. In fact, from my experience I believe that the reason a person acts the way he does in moments of pressure is because Satan (through wiles) will cause to come out of the id into the frontal lobe some hidden attitude that consumes the person for a moment and brings him into complete loss of control — for example, the powerful feelings of claustrophobia or perhaps, when as a child, being thrown into water and being unable to swim — from that moment on, locked in the mind is great fear of water (in some cases). There could be a great fear of heights. Many times on our trips to Israel, people have admitted their fear of flying. We had only to pray with them and break the bondage of that fear. They have never felt any fear again. The mind is marvelous. It never forgets. Therefore, these bondages or strongholds must be broken through prayer. I must urge you, when you pray, to pray directly to the Father and agree that the mind be cleansed.

Then I always reckon with God after the cleansing through prayer for the individual (Romans 12:1-2), and I know this sequence is backwards; however, I personally believe the mind is the foundation of all and must be dealt with to the pulling down of all strongholds in order that the life can be presented to Christ as a living sacrifice. I also reckon for the individual (Philippians 2:5), that there might be the mind of Christ through his life.

Then as we continue in this area of healing, we pray that the EMOTIONS might be healed. We ask for the peace of God to break into the life of the person that there might come deep inner peace and victory in his life — that God would develop His holy quietness in the person's life. We have seen many people with great problems brought to a calm presence with God.

And then pray for FULNESS. I personally believe that you can put prayer in the bank. That is, get a promise for the future, stand with it and God will honor it. I have already gotten a promise through prayer for my children and for my grandchildren and their futures. However, in dealing with those in this area, I pray, "Lord, I agree with You for what is written in heaven, for this individual for the rest of his life." I stay in that position of resistance until a release comes. Now what I have asked God for is the promise of Ephesians 2:10 (Amplified), that the individual might be brought to complete liberty in his life. I have asked God for a promise of His ministry to and through the person, and that Satan be bound. I personally believe this can be done; however, it is up to that individual to have a daily constant pursuit of the Lord in the activity of his own life. I know God has given me a promise for my family, and I have received many promises for those that we pray with. In essence, to pray with an individual, to break bondage in his life, you will need to pray regarding:

1. Breaking Genetic Ties
2. Negative Confession
3. Salvation
4. Deliverance
5. Healing
6. Fulness

Now I have saved the deliverance area to deal with last. Deliverance is dealing with all of those things by name that we listed earlier. When I pray for an individual in the area of deliverance, I begin first of all with the words that God gives intuitively in my mind. This is known as discernment and is listed in I Corinthians 12:10. Many times the Lord has allowed me to pray the exact problem of the individual by calling its name; thereby assuring them that I was receiving, through discernment, God's mind as to his need. Now, all of the things that I have listed in this writing are called out and demanded to leave: lust, guilt, pride, envy, hate, anger, jealousy, rage, rebellion, resentment, greed, fear, insecurity, inferiority, hostility, or any thought, act or deed of suicide, lying, cheating, lust of the flesh, lust of the eye, pride of life, sorcery, idolatry, witchcraft.

Many times you will receive other words to pray. However, in doing so, please be careful to have cleansed yourself and your mind in order that the intuition you receive is not your own or from another source other than the Holy Spirit. Also be very careful with the last items. Go very slowly in the area of the lust of the flesh, lust of the eye and pride of life. Wait for releases in these areas. They can include a multitude of sins. Then deal with sorcery on the basis of breaking the bondage of drugs, rock music or country and western music. Call these items out. Deal slowly with idolatry for this could mean money, position, family or anything that is put before God. And then with witchcraft, make sure you name the basic areas listed in Deuteronomy 18:9-14. Study this in several translations. Memorize these Scriptures, for it is in this area that the greatest bondage is found. God states in the Old Testament, "Rebellion is as the sin of witchcraft" (I Samuel 15:23). This area must be broken. Be careful in this area. If you do not win this battle, you could lose the whole war.

These areas must be dealt with as I pray with a person. Again, the bondage must be broken; therefore you stay in resistance until the liberty and the peace comes within. You are actually resisting the devil in each matter while receiving a release. When complete freedom is experienced you move on into the area of healing. God may lead you to change the sequence of this warfare and may even give you more insight as to the battle. Be sensitive to the Holy Spirit and He will guide you into all truth. Let me ask you to reread this chapter several times to establish yourself. Study also the Scripture references. Prepare yourself. No soldier is placed in battle without prior training. You, in Christ, are the first step to the deliverance. It must begin with you. Then you teach the person to retain his victory. Teach him to constantly pursue the Lord. He must be disciplined. As you have learned to do, teach him to fill his mind with Jesus; to come to a point of praise in everything. Teach him that we have all authority in Christ; that we are more than conquerors through Him. The Bible says that it is through the blood of Jesus that not only are we brought to liberty, but the Christian can have the privilege of bringing liberty to others. Satan is a defeated foe. His defeat is in the past tense. He is overcome. We are overcomers.

As you grow in grace and knowledge and are brought to victory, you can not only be liberated in your own heart, but you can bring liberation to others. Again, study this book carefully. Bring yourself to such oneness with Christ that you are liberated and then be a champion for Christ in the area of spiritual warfare. Do not enter into this lightly. Begin by prayer and then seek God's authority to minister to others. To begin with, here are Scriptures I encourage you to memorize (you encourage others to memorize them that they, too, might be liberated and retain their liberation):

Revelation 12:10-11
Colossians 2:15
I John 3:8
Mark 11:23
James 4:7
Psalm 149:8-9

II Corinthians 10:4-5
Luke 10:17-19
I John 4:4
I John 5:4
Hebrews 2:14-15
II Corinthians 2:14
Joel 2:32
I Corinthians 15:57
Isaiah 54:17
Jeremiah 1:19

These verses will help you retain your victory in Christ and bring liberty to others. God bless you. Be faithful even unto death.

In further study, I recommend other tapes or books I have ministered in. If you have problems in the area of

(1) Forgetting or forgiving
  a. Book — *God Can Heal Your Mind*
  b. Tape Series — God Can Heal Your Mind (7 Tapes)

(2) Negative confession or gossip
  a. Book — *Death and Life Are in the Tongue*

(3) Spiritual warfare (Satan and Demons)
  a. Book — *Spiritual Warfare Manual*
  b. Book — *Deliverance, the Children's Bread*
  c. Tapes — Satan Series (16 tapes on How to Combat Satan and Have Personal Deliverance)

(4) How to have answered prayer
  a. Book — *Prayer is Warfare*

  b. Tapes — How to Have Answered Prayer (6 Tapes)
  c. Tapes — How to Come to a Life of Faith (6 Tapes)

(5) How to begin and have a Christian home
  a. Book — *What's Wrong With America?*
  b. Tapes — Home Series (12 Tapes)

(6) Getting out of debt
   a. Book — *Scriptural Way to Get Out of Debt*

(7) Gifts of the Spirit
   a. Tapes — How to Discover Your Spiritual Gift (4 Tapes)

(8) How to find God's will for your life
   a. Book — *How to Find God's Will for Your Life*

Order from
Mickey Bonner Evangelistic Association
P.O. Box 90593
Houston, Texas 77290